5-D

How to See the Hidden 5-D™ Stereogram Image

Hold the art close to your nose so that it appears blurry. Relax your eyes and stare at the artwork. Make believe you are looking "through" the art. Slowly move the artwork away from your face until the hidden Multi-Dimensional image resolves into perfect clarity. The time it takes to see the image can vary, so don't get discouraged!

Alternate viewing method: Place a sheet of plastic or glass over the page so that you can see your own reflection. Hold the art at arm's length and focus on your reflection in the plastic or glass until the 5-D™ stereogram image resolves into perfect clarity.

If you are still unable to see the images, pictures of the hidden 5-D™ stereogram images can be found at the end of this book.

Important: If you experience any discomfort, stop, rest, and try again later.

SPORTS
in 5-D™ Stereograms

Created by Stephen Schutz, Ph.D.,
and Susan Polis Schutz

Every illustration in this book
has a hidden 5-D™ stereogram picture
waiting to be discovered by you.

Boulder, Colorado

Mail Order

Other exciting 5-D™ products available from Blue Mountain Press:

- Greeting Cards
- Prints (11" x 14")
- Books:
  - Endangered Species in 5-D™ Stereograms
  - Love in 5-D™ Stereograms
  - Reach for Your Dreams in 5-D™ Stereograms
  - Sea Life in 5-D™ Stereograms
- Calendars:
  - Endangered Species in 5-D™ Stereograms
  - Sea Life in 5-D™ Stereograms
  - Sports in 5-D™ Stereograms

For ordering information, please contact us at:

Blue Mountain Press
Mail Order
P.O. Box 4549
Boulder, Colorado 80306
(303) 449-0536

The following people are to be thanked for their valuable contribution to this book: Faith Gowan, Peter Kay, Patty Brown, Ed Guzik, Mark Rinella, Matt Rantanen, and Jared Schutz.

Quote by Greg Noll excerpted from **Da Bull: Life over the Edge** by Greg Noll (Berkeley, CA: North Atlantic Books, 1989). Used by permission.

Thanks to **SNOWBOARDER Magazine** for permission to reprint the quote by Jamie Lynn, and to International Management Group for permission to reprint the quote by Arnold Palmer.

"The dreams that a true athlete has..." by Dena Dilaconi is copyright © 1995 by Dena Dilaconi. Used by permission.

design on book cover is registered in U.S. Patent and Trademark Office

ISBN: 0-88396-413-9

Printed in Hong Kong
First Printing: March, 1995

P.O. Box 4549, Boulder, Colorado 80306

Introduction

Today, hundreds of millions of people around the world have fun participating in sports as athletes or spectators. In this respect, sports truly has become the universal language of mankind. Events from Little League to the Olympics are occasions for people to celebrate the things that unite human beings rather than divide them, as well as honor and recognize the highest ideals of human endeavor. To have a goal and then to devote every resource of imagination, determination, and desire to attain it — this is the real foundation of sports, and of every dream in life.

Sports in 5-D™ Stereograms reveals magical hidden images that are as exciting as the sports that it honors.

Football

"Football embodies the spirit of America... power, strength, and teamwork. Football is the ultimate team game, as all eleven players have to work as one for team success."

— Pat Bowlen
Owner, Denver Broncos

5-D™ Stereogram Image: **"The Big Game"**

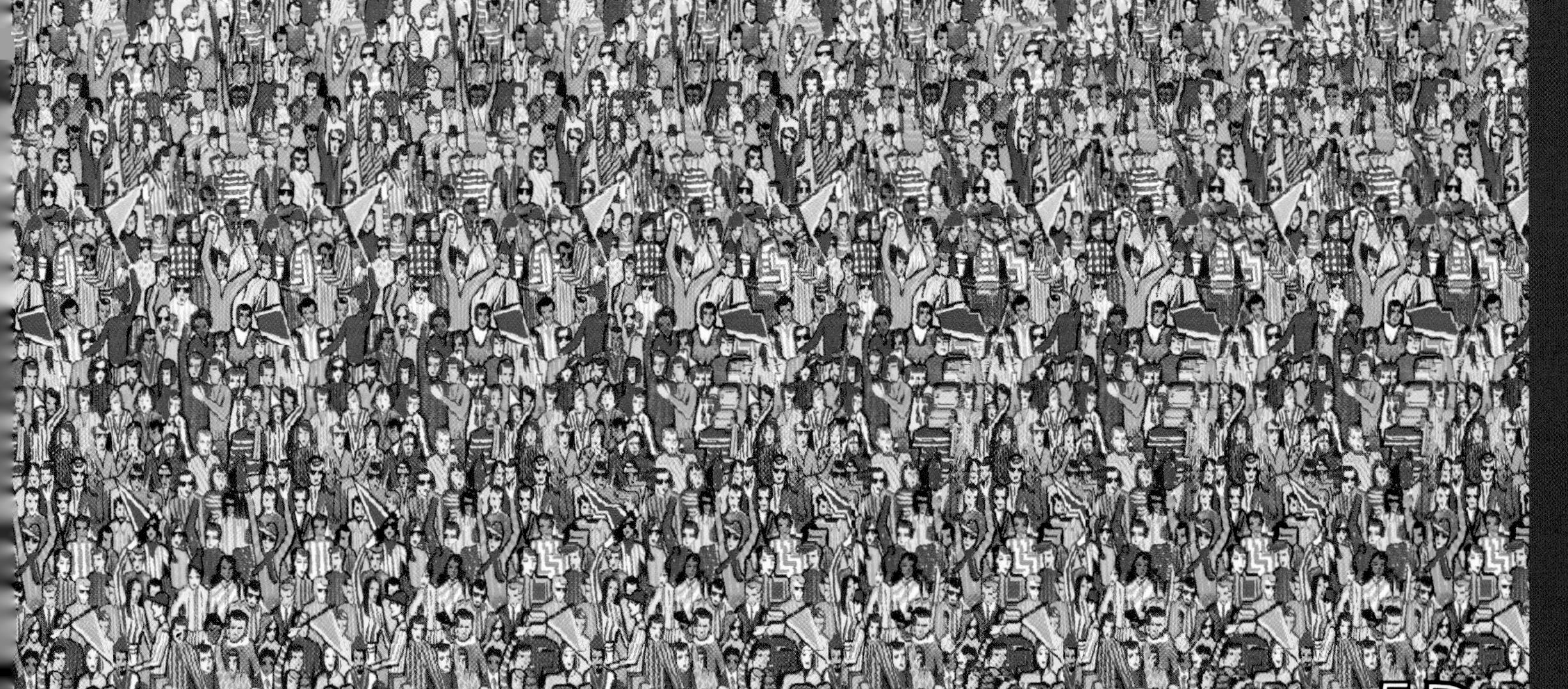
5D™

Basketball

"To me, basketball is a form of art. If all goes as choreographed, individual physical talent blended with superb team cohesion result in spectacular plays that can never be duplicated."

— Ceal Barry
University of Colorado
Women's Head Basketball Coach

5-D™ Stereogram Image: **"Basketball Player"**

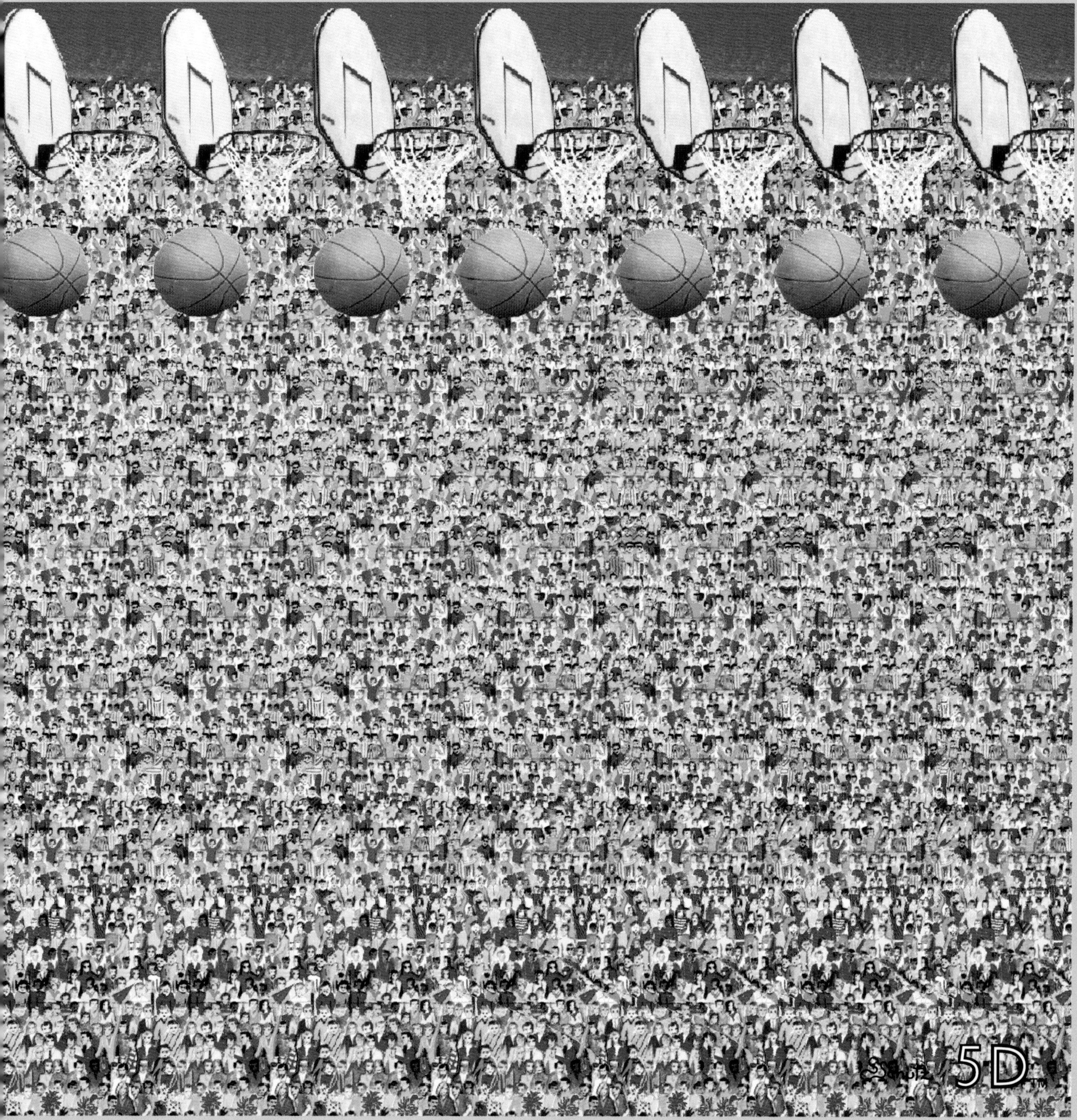

5D™

Baseball

*For over a century,
baseball has traditionally been known
as "America's Favorite Pastime."*

"Baseball reveals true character, and creates respect and discipline within the person and the team."

— Ernie Banks
Mr. Cub®

5-D™ Stereogram Image: **"Home Run"**

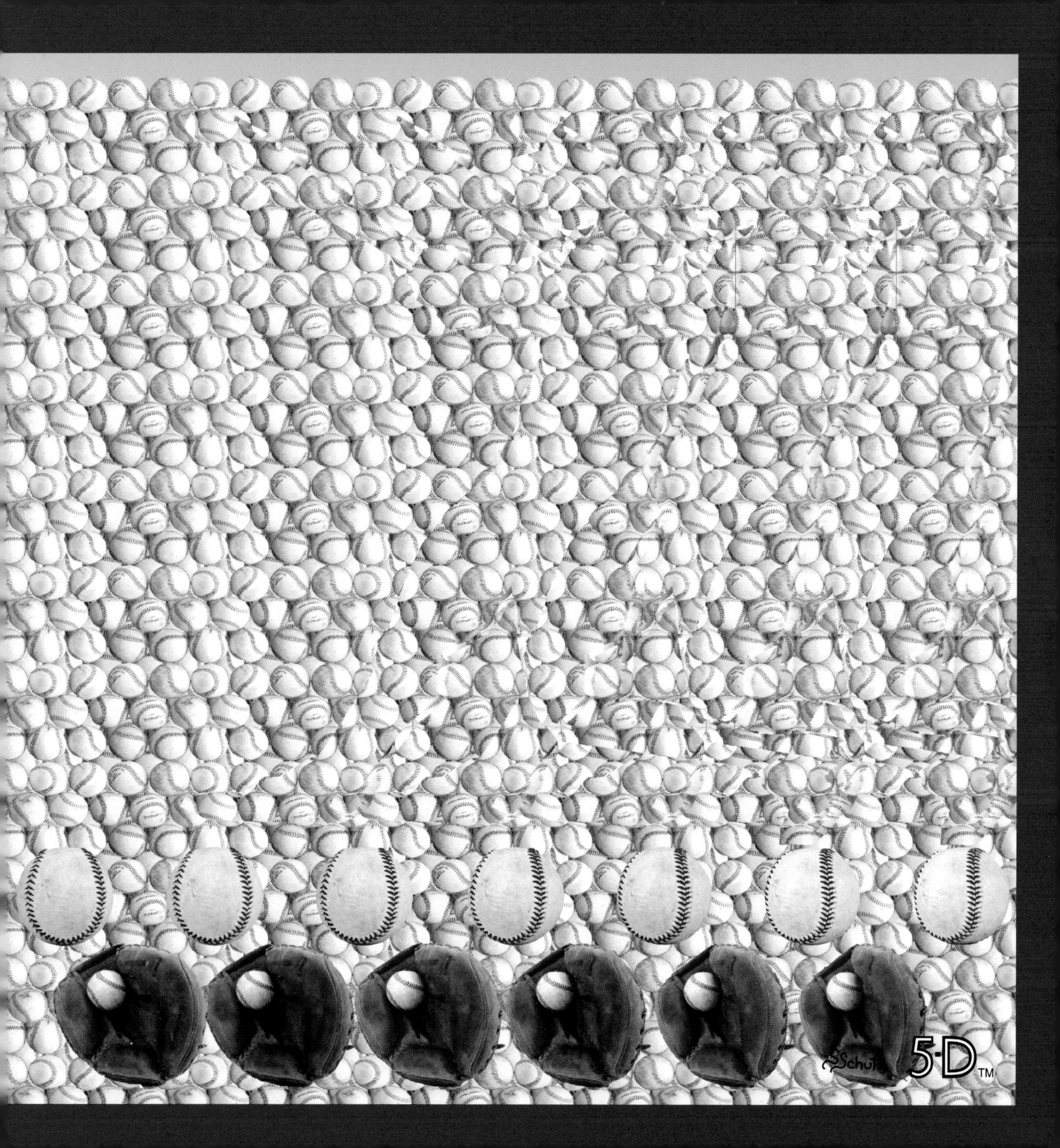
5-D

Soccer

Soccer is a showcase for many of the finest elements in all competitive sports. The game progresses in almost-constant motion, flowing from one moment to the next in an interweaving of action, color, and dramatic plays full of excitement and suspense. Intricate teamwork is punctuated by flashes of individual brilliance. It's easy to understand why hundreds of millions of fans and players love this game so much.

5-D™ Stereogram Image: **"Soccer Star"**

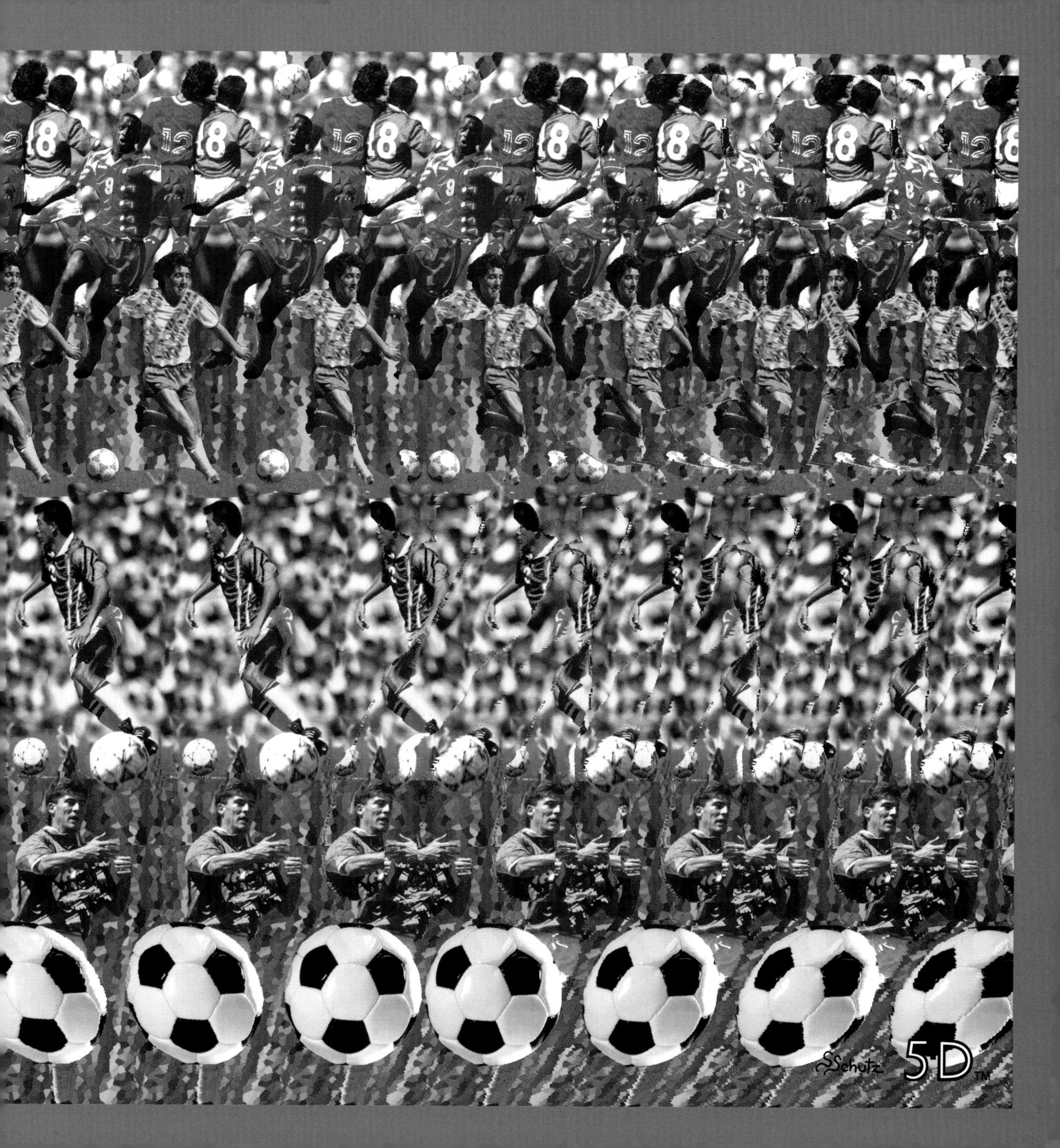
Schutz
5D TM

Tennis

"Tennis is one of the most exactingly difficult disciplines in sports. Combining its unique scoring system with the technical difficulty of timing a moving object and redirecting its flight accurately is a lifelong challenge. Given the general history of most competitive sports, it is refreshing to be rewarded for being consistent and just getting the ball back 'one more time'!"

— Art Thomson
USPTA Tennis Professional;
1993 National Player of the Year
for Teaching Professionals

5-D™ Stereogram Image: **"Tennis Player"**

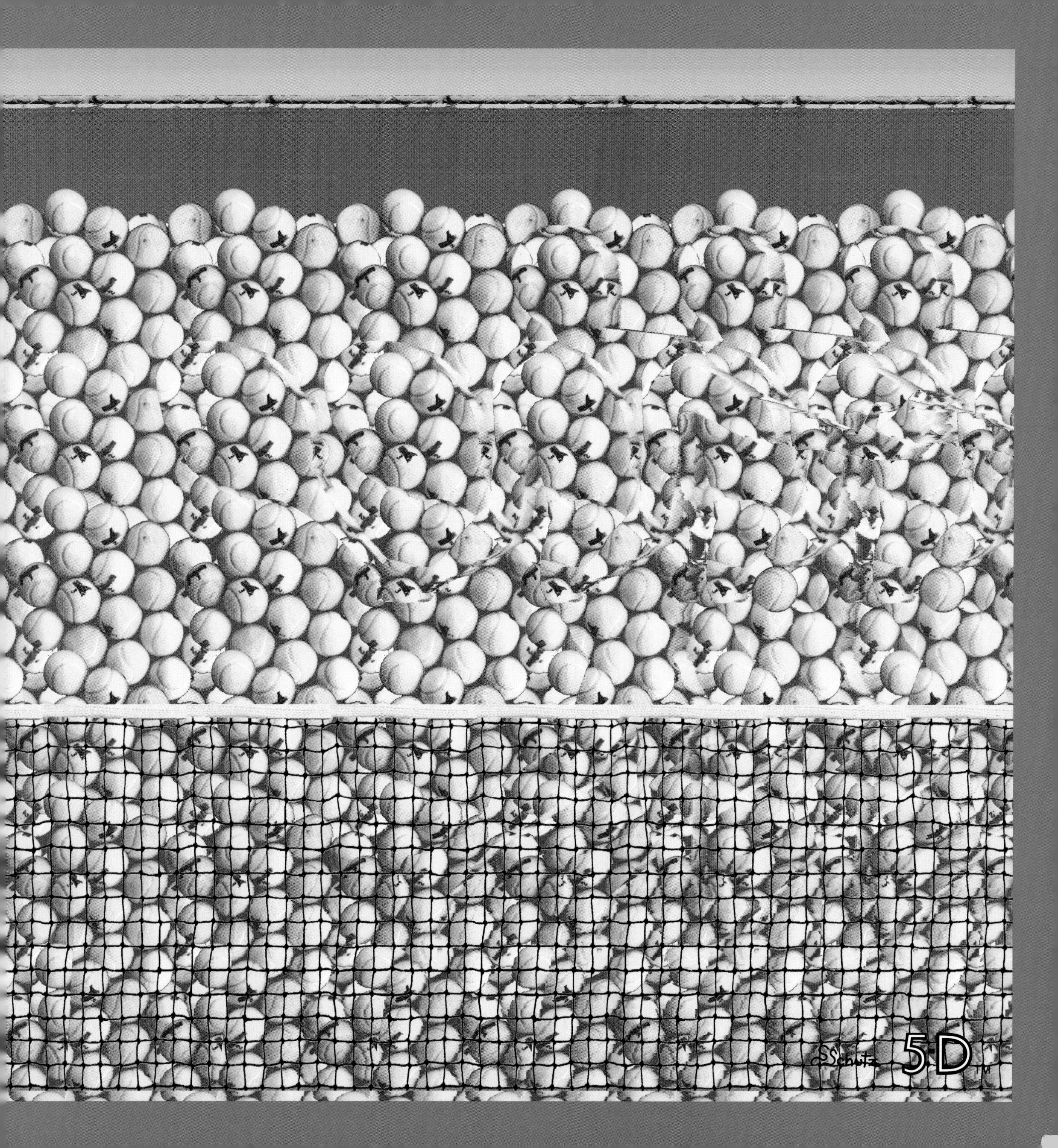
5D

Surfing

"There's something really magnetic about the ocean. I think if I live to be eighty, I'll never forget some of my first times surfing, where the first glimpse that I got of the ocean each day would be reflected in my attitude for the rest of the day."

— Greg Noll
Pioneer Big-Wave Surfer

5-D™ Stereogram Image: **"Surfer"**

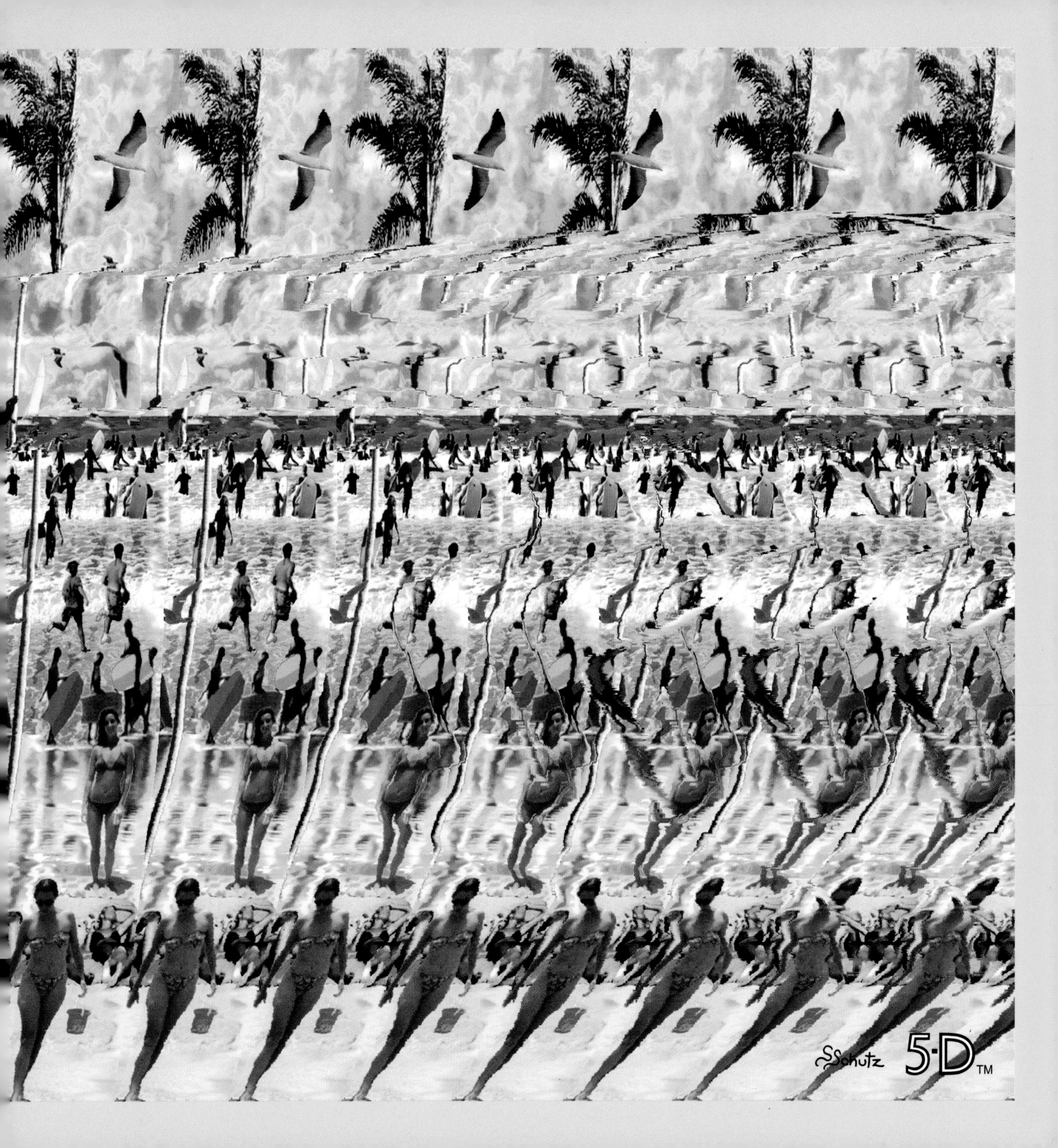
Schutz
5-D
TM

Fishing

"Fishing is enjoyed by millions because it offers something for everyone. If you want a solitary experience, you can have it. If you want a competitive endeavor, you can have that. Fishing is whatever you want to make it."

— Steve Pennaz
Executive Director, North American Fishing Club;
Editor, *North American Fishing Magazine*

5-D™ Stereogram Image: **"Catching a Fish"**

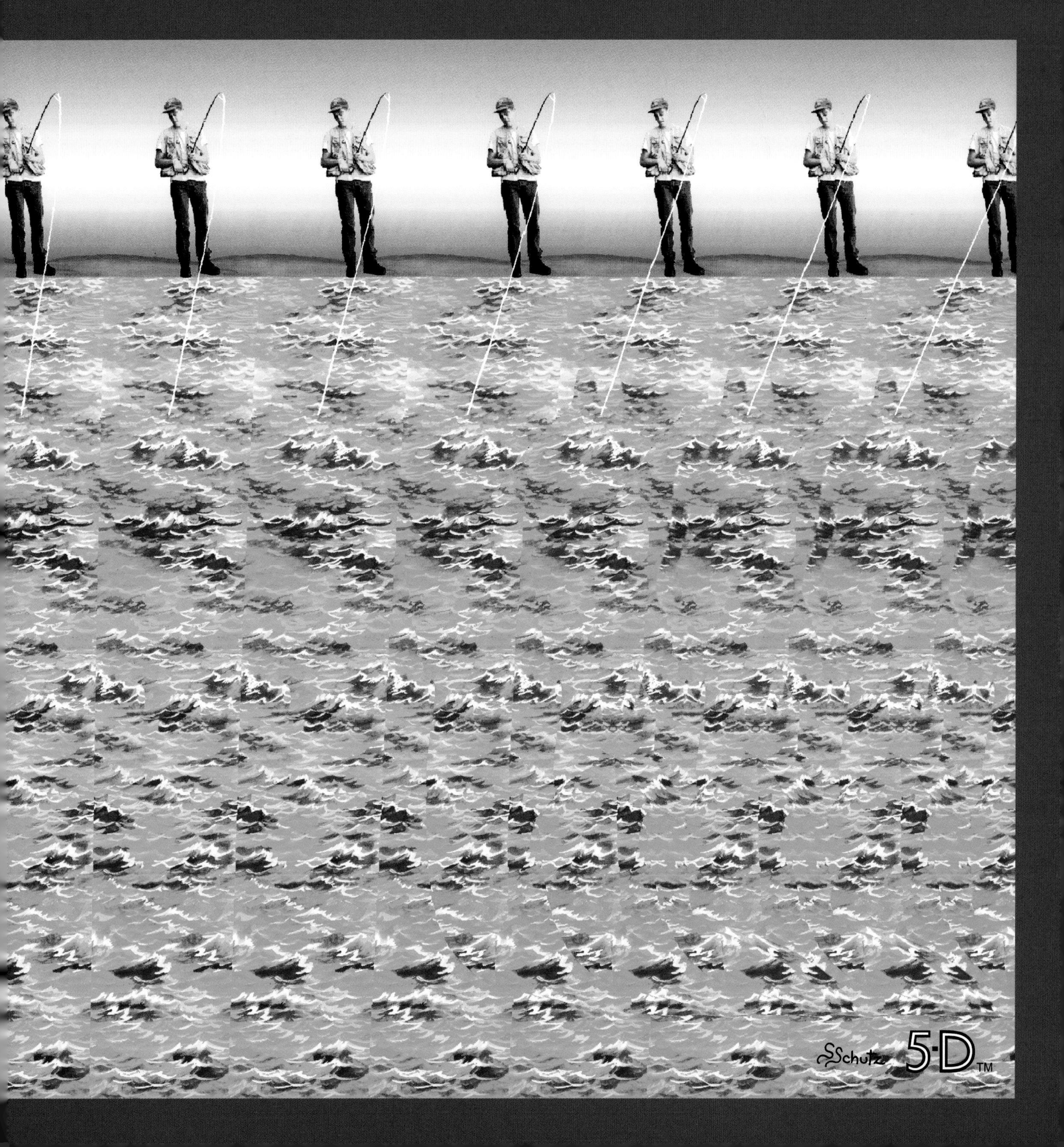
SSchutz
5-D™

Golf

"Golf is deceptively simple and endlessly complicated. A child can play it well and a grown man can never master it. Any single round of it is full of unexpected triumphs and perfect shots that end in disaster. It is almost a science, yet it is a puzzle without an answer. It is gratifying and tantalizing, precise and unpredictable; it requires complete concentration and total relaxation. It satisfies the soul and frustrates the intellect. It is at the same time rewarding and maddening — and it is without doubt the greatest game mankind has ever invented."

— Arnold Palmer
Professional Golfer;
Winner of 60 PGA Tour Events
and Eight Major Championships

5-D™ Stereogram Image: **"Driving the Green"**

SSchutz
5D TM

Cycling

"The wind in your face on a sunny day, miles of road before you and behind you. This is the joy of cycling.

"You see things from your bike that you don't see by car, because you ride more slowly, giving you more time to absorb the nuances of the environment. You gain endurance and strength, certainly, but primarily cycling gives clarity of thought, an escape from the noisy, distracting world that we live in. Cycling develops your body and relaxes your mind.

"More than anything, riding a bike brings you into the here and now, because your attention is mainly on the moment, forcing you to be part of the moment. By being so involved, you can set your thoughts free and unburden yourself. This is the gift of cycling."

— Connie Carpenter
Olympic Gold Medalist, Cycling

5-D™ Stereogram Image: **"Gearing Up"**

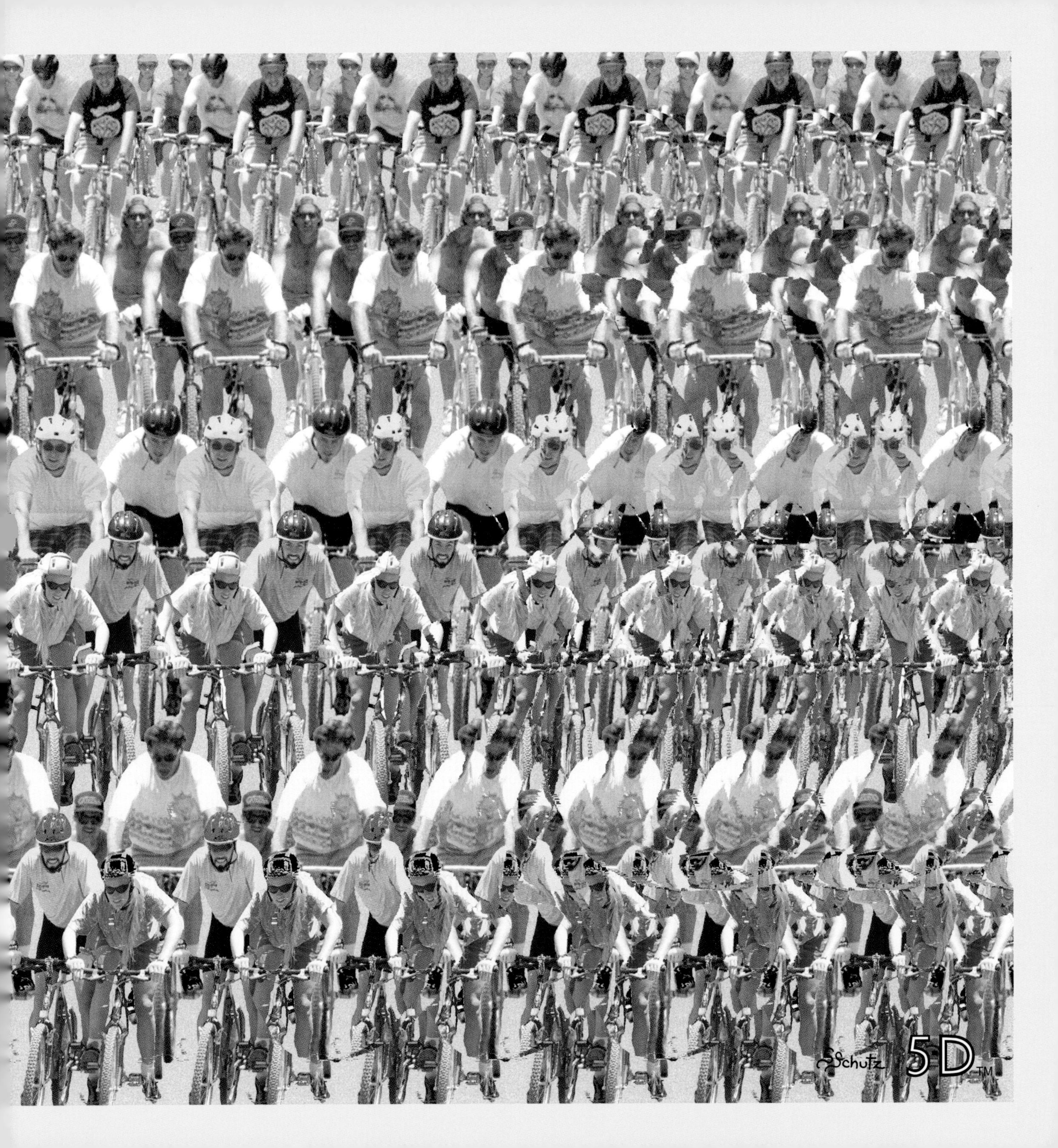
Schutz
5D TM

Ice Hockey

Hockey is team sport cranked to maximum intensity. Take twelve extreme competitors flashing across the ice at thirty miles an hour. Throw in the brilliant overhead lights glaring off the ice, the sound of sharp skates scraping the ice, the crack of sticks tangling, the roar of the fans, and players flying onto and off the ice in the middle of the action. It all adds up to a glorious experience in sensory overload that no other sport can offer.

5-D™ Stereogram Image: "**Slap Shot**"

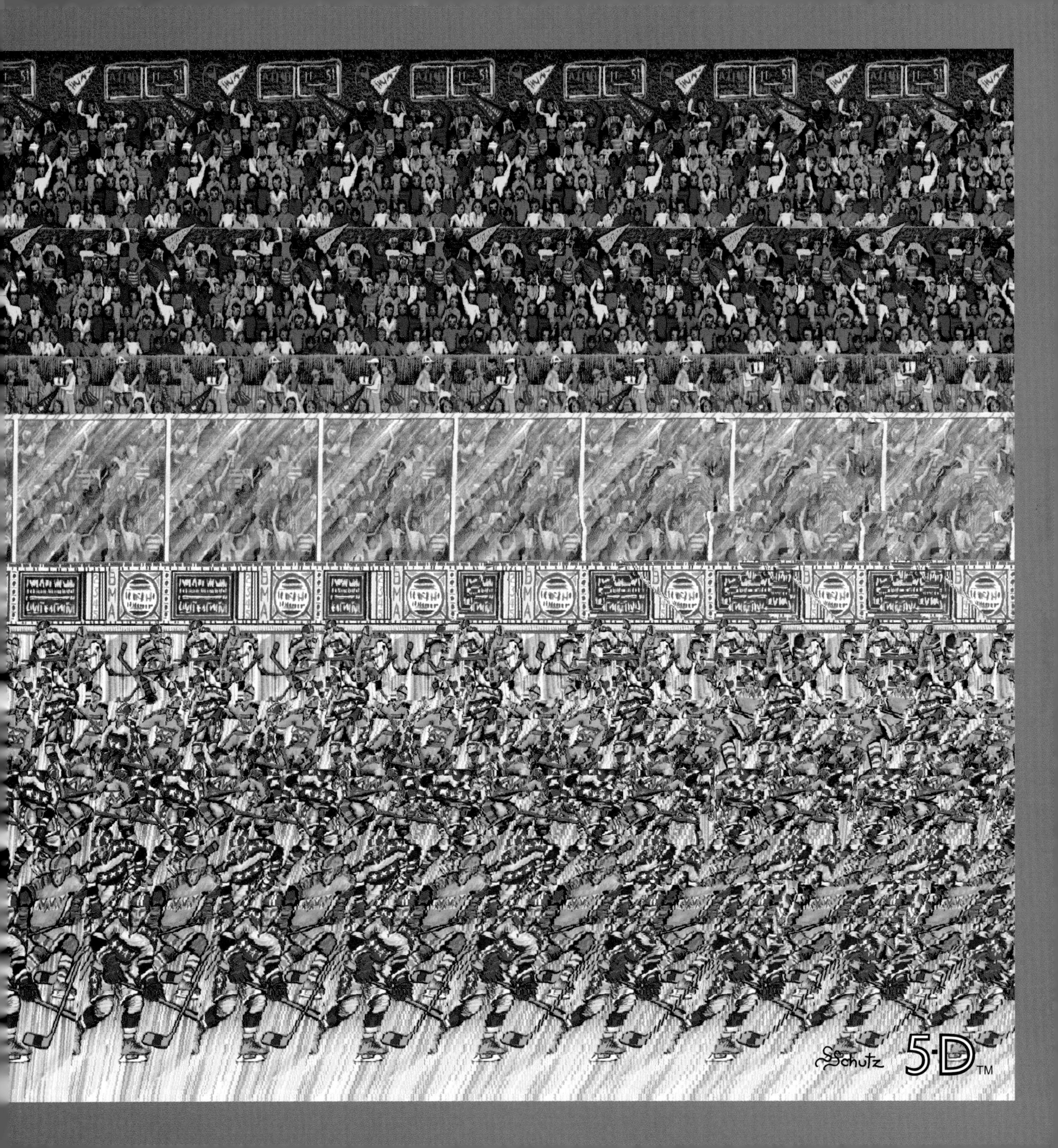
Schutz
5-D TM

Snowboarding

"Snowboarding is such a fun sport. It's grown so much in the past years... The main point is going out and just doing it for fun and doing it for yourself because you love it so much you wouldn't want to do anything else."

— Jamie Lynn
World-Class Snowboarder

5-D™ Stereogram Image: **"Shredder"**

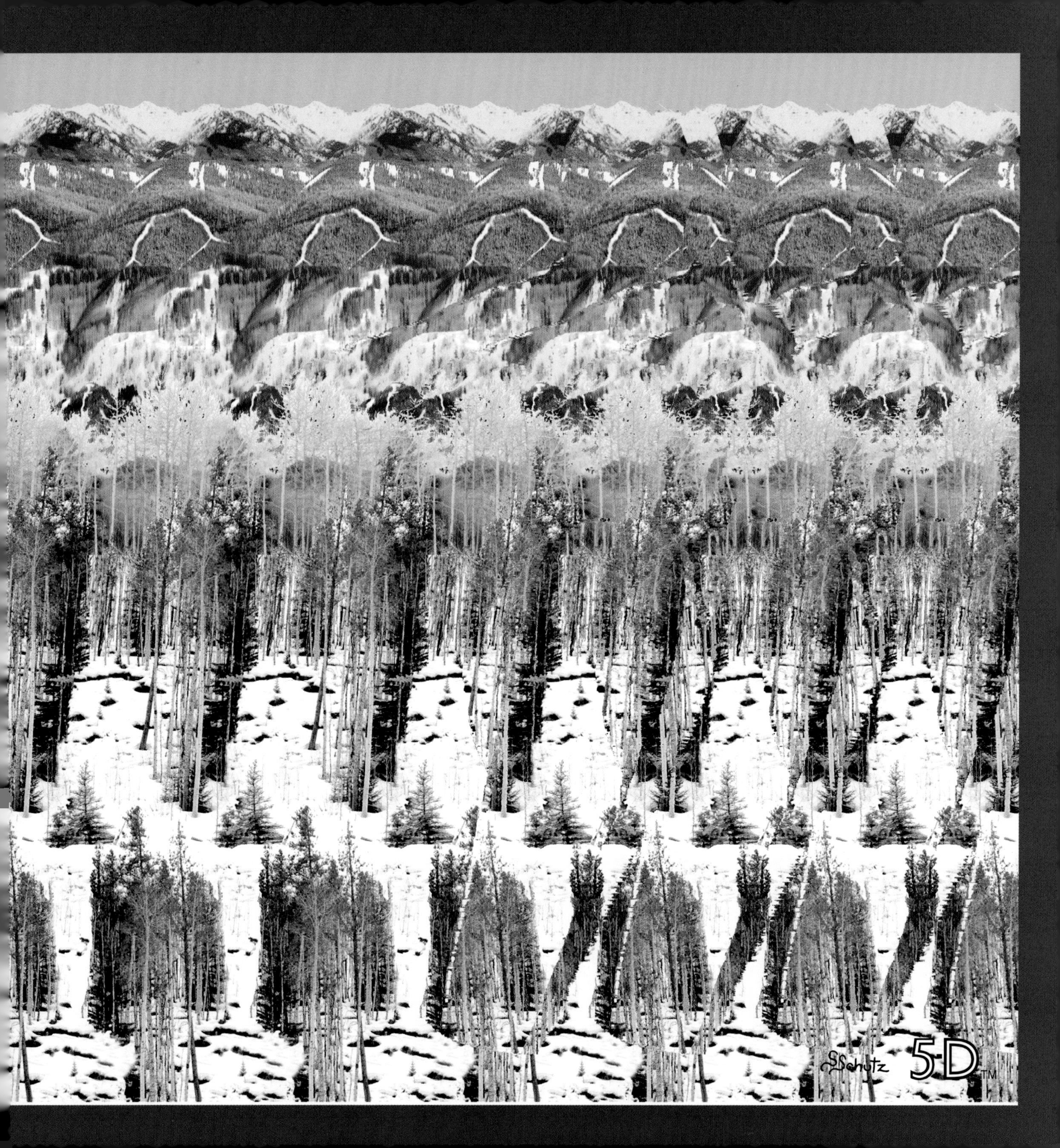
SSchutz
5D™

Skiing

"Skiing appeals to me for a wide variety of reasons. My background is racing... my passion is powder...

"The only constant in skiing is the color of the snow. Everything else is a variable. If you want adrenaline, there's the downhill; if you want precision, you have the slalom. Every mountain is different, and there are beautiful mountains all over the world.

"Skiing appeals to everyone, from two-year-old kids to people in their eighties. They come from cities and towns and out in the country, from all walks of life. It's the kind of sport you get hooked on the very first time — and once you try it, you'll become a skier for life."

— Billy Kidd
1st American man to win a medal
in Olympic skiing;
1st American man to win a gold medal
at the World Alpine Championships

5-D™ Stereogram Image: **"First Tracks"**

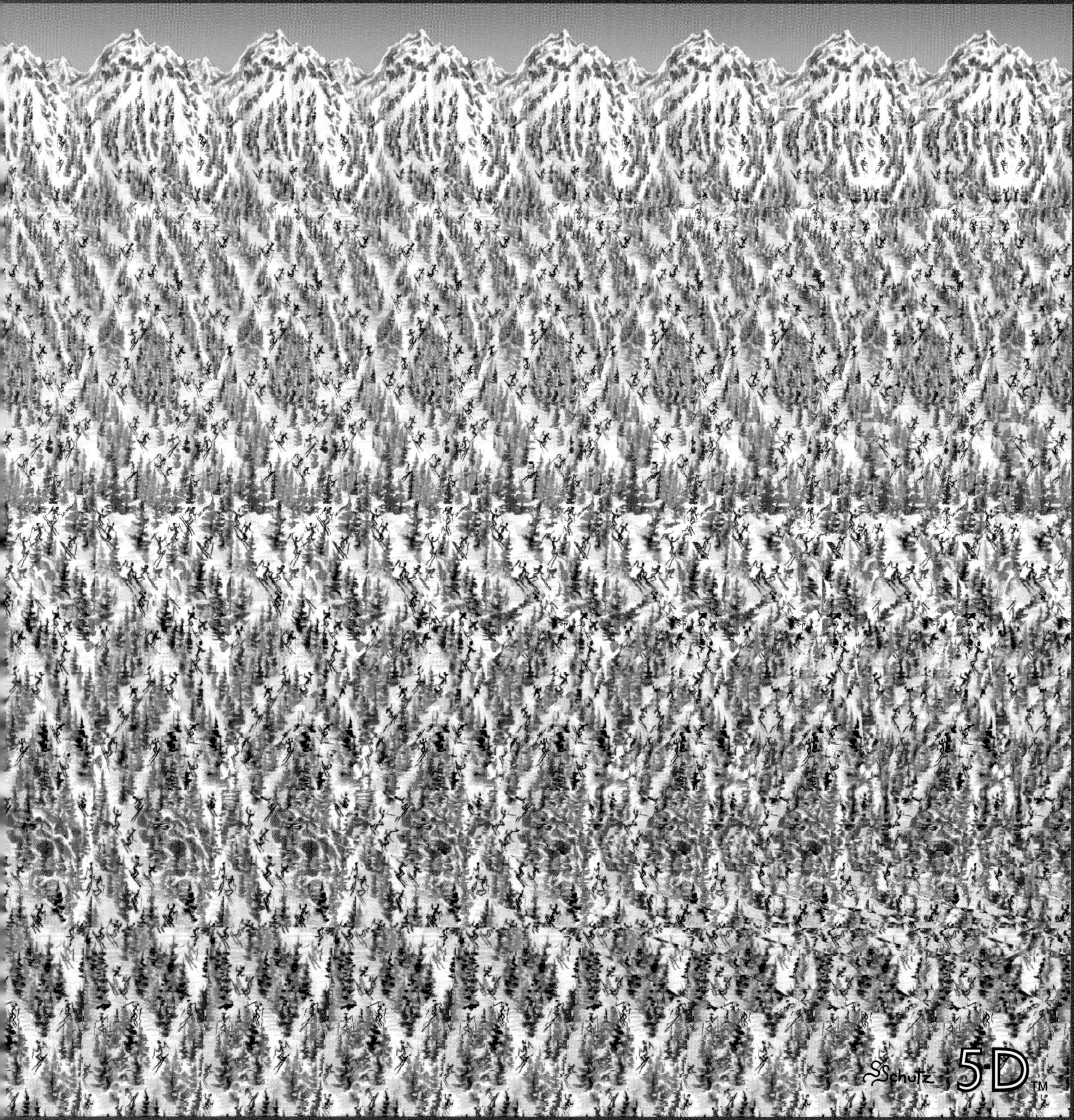

Schutz 5D™

The dreams that a true athlete has
are ones of personal satisfaction
and pride.
They are the distant hopes
of competition
that only lead them further
down the road
towards other challenges and rewards.

5-D™ Stereogram Image: **“Drive to the Hoop”**

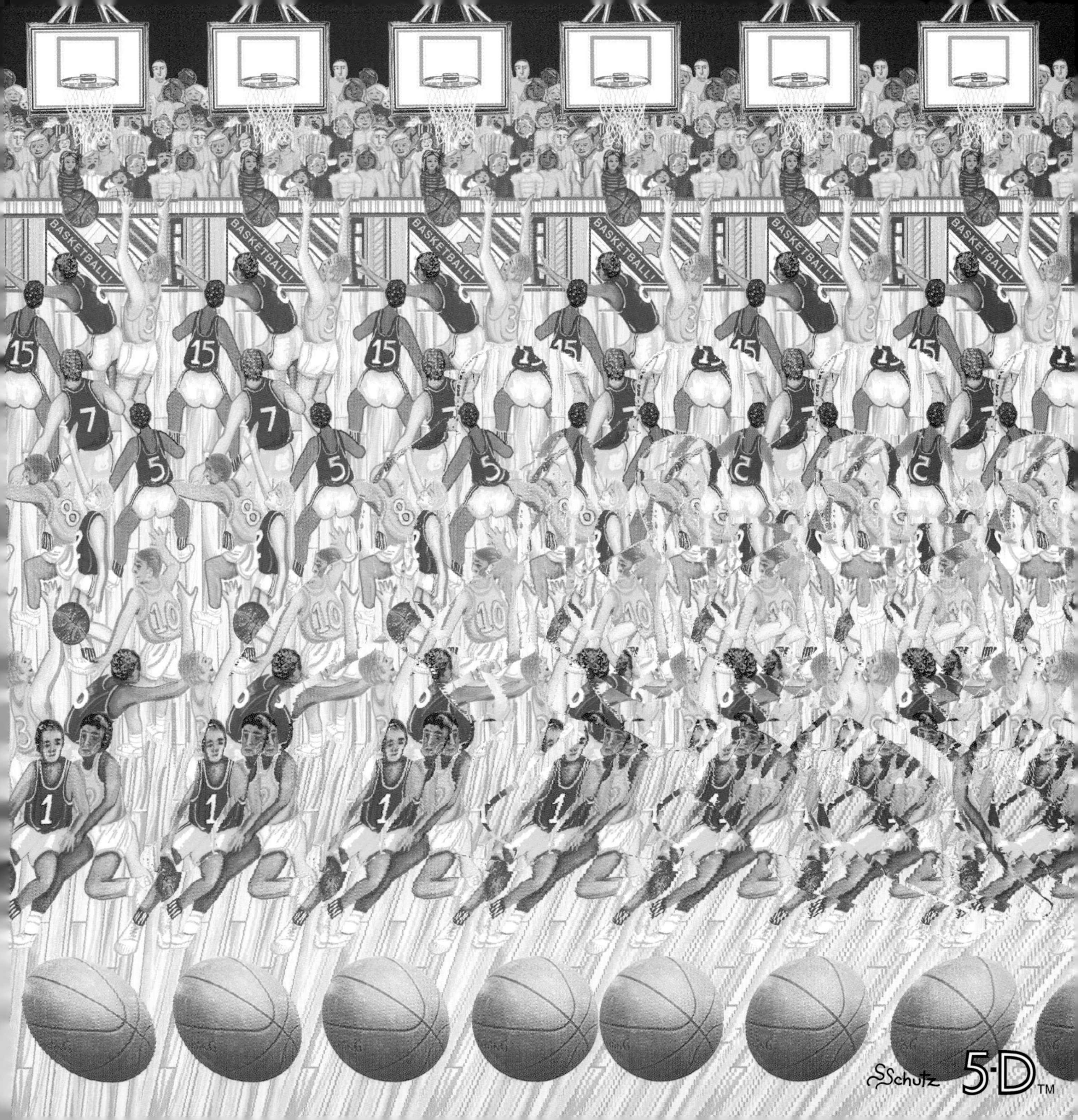
BASKETBALL!
SSchutz
5-D TM

Seeing in Stereo

Stephen Schutz, Ph.D., Takes the Art of the Stereogram to a New Aesthetic Level

Recent improvements in computer technology have enabled the famous artist (and physicist) Stephen Schutz to pass a new threshold of innovation and liberate art from its prior two-dimensional limitations. "Spectacular!" says Leonard Nimoy about 5-D™ stereograms. "Beautiful and often dazzling works of art," says Dick Kreck of *The Denver Post*.

5-D™ stereograms, Stephen Schutz's most recent artistic creation, effectively establish a genre of Multi-Dimensional art. Stereograms had their origins in 1960 when Bela Julesz developed the "random-dot stereogram" as a tool to study perceptual psychology. For the past thirty years, primitive random-dot stereograms have relied on repetitive textures to disguise hidden three-dimensional images.

Stephen Schutz's 5-D™ stereograms have successfully replaced random-dot textures with incredible artwork, which makes 5-D™ stereograms "dimensional dynamite," in the words of David Hutchison of the National Stereoscopic Association. The full-color base-art foregrounds (what everyone sees on the surface) are attractions in and of themselves. When this foreground is dramatically supplemented by a hidden image that relates and interacts with it, the exquisite result comes alive as basketball players leap off the page and a golfer appears in mid-swing. Stephen Schutz's accomplishment is a testimony to what can happen when the creative envelope of art is expanded and enhanced by the cutting edge of technology.

"Over the past few years, random-dot stereograms have been popping up all over the place. Unfortunately, most are very boring," notes 3-D collector and writer for *Stereo World* magazine, Sheldon Aronowitz. "This has all changed with the release of the Blue Mountain Arts 5-D™ stereograms developed by Dr. Stephen Schutz. In their flat format, they are works of art in their own right. When viewed in three dimensions, you will be amazed and delighted with the clarity and ingenious blending of theme. No more patterns of endless dots."

About the Artist and Author

Stephen Schutz is an artist and a physicist, a rare combination of talents emanating from the mind and heart. Enraptured at an early age with beauty and aesthetic form, Stephen pursued the paths of science and art simultaneously. He graduated from the famous High School of Music and Art in New York, and studied physics at M.I.T. and Princeton University, where he received a Ph.D. in theoretical physics in 1970. While pursuing advanced scientific learning, Stephen continued to develop his artistic abilities at the Museum of Fine Arts in Boston.

During college, Stephen met and fell in love with the woman who was to become his equal loving partner in marriage, family, and art. In 1969, Susan Polis Schutz and Stephen Schutz moved to the mountains of Colorado where Susan was a freelance writer and Stephen researched solar energy at a government research laboratory. On the weekends, they began experimenting with printing Susan's poems surrounded by Stephen's art on posters that they silk-screened in their basement. From the very start, their love of life and for one another touched a receptive chord in people everywhere. The public's discovery of the creative collaboration of Susan Polis Schutz and Stephen Schutz set the stage for a world-wide love affair with their works. Frequent visitors to the bestseller lists, Susan and Stephen's books and poetry cards have touched the hearts of over 200 million people, and their works have been translated into many languages.

Because Stephen is an artist, computer whiz, and innovator, there is no one better suited to take the art of the stereogram to its next level. Combine that with the fact that it would be difficult to discover a poet with a more significant following than Susan Polis Schutz, who *TIME* magazine referred to as "the reigning star... in high emotion." Together, Susan and Stephen Schutz's most recent books, featuring Susan's poetic messages and Stephen's 5-D™ stereograms, are just the latest in a series of beautiful contributions the couple has made over the past 25 years.

Hidden 5-D™ Stereogram Images

The Big Game

Basketball Player

Home Run

Soccer Star

Tennis Player

Surfer

Catching a Fish

Driving the Green

Gearing Up

Slap Shot

Shredder

First Tracks

Drive to the Hoop

5-D
Schutz